LOAD IN
NINE TIMES

LOAD IN NINE TIMES

POEMS

Frank X Walker

Liveright Publishing Corporation

A Division of W. W. Norton & Company
Independent Publishers Since 1923

For information about permission to reproduce selections from this book,
write to Permissions, Liveright Publishing Corporation, a division of
W. W. Norton & Company, Inc., 500 Fifth Avenue, New York, N.Y. 10110

For information about special discounts for bulk purchases, please contact
W. W. Norton Special Sales at specialsales@wwnorton.com or 800-233-4830

Manufacturing by Versa Press
Book design by Beth Steidle
Production manager: Lauren Abbate

ISBN 978-1-324-09493-7

Liveright Publishing Corporation, 500 Fifth Avenue, New York, N.Y. 10110
www.wwnorton.com

W. W. Norton & Company Ltd., 15 Carlisle Street, London W1D 3BS

1 2 3 4 5 6 7 8 9 0

*For my ancestors, Mary and Randal
Edelen, 125th U.S. Colored Infantry
and Elvira and Henry Clay Walker,
12th U.S. Colored Troops Heavy Artillery*

" . . . we fight for men and women
whose poetry is not yet written."

—CAPT. ROBERT GOULD SHAW,
54TH MASSACHUSETTS

"How long have I in bondage lain,
And languished to be free!
Alas! and must I still complain—
Deprived of liberty."

—FROM GEORGE MOSES HORTON'S POEM
"ON LIBERTY AND SLAVERY"

"So all honor and all glory
    To those noble sons of Ham—
The gallant colored soldiers
    Who fought for Uncle Sam!"

—FROM PAUL LAURENCE DUNBAR'S
POEM "THE COLORED SOLDIER"

CONTENTS

PART I

PART II

PART III

LOAD IN
NINE TIMES

$30 Reward!

RANAWAY from the subscriber (in Henderson county, N. C.,) on the night of the 3d inst., a NEGRO BOY named

GEORGE.

He carried with him Two Hundred and Thirty-Seven Dollars in silver coin, and is supposed to be accompanied by some trifling white person, (probably a suspicious looking woman.) The above reward of Thirty Dollars will be paid for the apprehension and confinement of George in any jail in the United States, so that I get him and the money—or Ten Dollars for the negro without the money—or Twenty Dollars for the recovery of all the money without the negro.

Description.

GEORGE is near six feet high; of a black, rough complexion; talks a little soft, or broken; affects to be witty; and is rather insolent or careless in conversation. The middle finger on his left hand, I think, is stiff, and probably a large scar on the great toe of his left foot, near the insertion of the nail, occasioned by the cut of an axe, and the end of the toe pointed downwards. Had on when he left home, a new cotton and tow shirt and pantaloons, an old wool hat, and linsey jacket; but as he has the funds necessary with him, he will probably change his clothing the first opportunity.

Communications on the subject to be addressed to L. S. GASH, Claytonville, Henderson county, North Carolina.

June 11, 1841.   REUBEN JOHNSON,
                                 tf   52

☞ The Register, at Knoxville, Ten., and the Mountaineer, at Greenville, S. C., will each give the above four insertions, and forward their accounts to the Post Master at Claytonville, or to this office, for collection.

Twenty Dollars Reward!

RAN away from the subscriber, or was conveyed away, on the night of the 27th of May,

A Negro Girl, named Fatima,

and her TWO CHILDREN, *Rufus* and *Rachel.* FATIMA is a bright mulatto girl, about five feet three or four inches high. Rufus is about 5 years old, rather darker than his mother. Rachel is about 2 years old, and a very bright mulatto.

The subscriber will give the above reward for said Negroes, delivered at his residence at D. W. Greenlee's.

JAMES M. GREENLEE.
Burke county, June 2, 1841.   3   52

I

"The sun shines bright on my old Kentucky home,
'Tis summer, the darkies are gay . . ."

—ORIGINAL LYRICS TO "MY OLD
    KENTUCKY HOME"

TRUTH BE TOLD

after Natasha Trethewey

Kentuckians, I believe, remember
too much of former selves—another life.
Antique stores line our main streets and broadways,
so many interactions swell with aches
older than the moment, violence erupts
with so little provocation, old wounds
fester, scores are settled not forgiven.
Whichever ancestor's blood speaks loudest
seems to govern our passions when we meet.
Yet generational traumas stay hushed,
minds are set firm around color and class,
mob behavior, and guns—always the guns.
It is as if so much blood was spilled here
our most sacred ground is still dark   and wet.

BACK SIDE OF MY OLD KENTUCKY HOME

at our estates
we sat on the side porch
stared at humble cabins

on horse farms
we sipped mint juleps
looked out over the hills

as young bucks
worked and sweated in the fields
and sang and danced

rode our thoroughbreds
raced each other in the meadows
to earn Sundays off to eat

we could smell
sour mash and brandies
and cast-iron skillets full of
nothing but love

the best fried chicken
cooked in large kettles and pots
seasoned genius
in every dish

those were good ol' days
breaking them
was more Christian
than selling them

for owners and families
carefully breeding them
was more profitable
on the auction block

AIN'T NO PLANTATIONS IN KENTUCKY

... unless you count Alexander Plantation House, Anatok, Anderson-Smith House, Arcadia, Ashland, Aspen Hall, Beechland, Blossom Hill, Blue Wing Landing, Cedars, Clay Hill, Coleman-Desha, Doricham, Duncan Hall, Edgewood, Elmwood, Emmick, Fairfax, Fairfield, Farmington, Fern Hill, Fishpool, Federal Grove, Federal Hill, Forest Hill, Gatliff, Giltner, Grange, Helm Place, Henry Duncan House, Honeysuckle Hill, Huston, James W. Alcorn House, Locust Grove, Longview Farm, Maple Hill Manor, Maplewood, three McClaskey plantations, McCutcheon Meadows, Mount Brilliant, Mount Lebanon, Newell B. McClaskey House, Oaklawn, Oldham, Oxmoor, Pleasant Retreat, Preston, Richwood, Ridgeway, Riverside, Rocky Hill, Sanford Bishop House, Scarlett Berkley Duncan, Slead House, Sportsman's Hill, Springfield, Springrest, Stillwell Heady, Stonehall, Sutfield House, Villa Lawn, W. J. Kendrick, Walnut Groves, Walnut Hill, Ward Hall, Waveland, Whitehall House, Wickland, William Gatewood, and Woodstock.

ACCOUNTING

To the man keeping the ledger
our *age*, our *sex*, and our *color*
was more important
than our names.

He counted 48 a us
from 6 full moons to 60 winters,
including 4 fugitives
from the state a Virginny.

The good news:
Alla us can hear and see,
and be mostly in our right minds.

The bad news:
Alla us be property
a Matilda Burks.

TESTIFY

*"The faded faces of the Negro children tell too plainly to
what degradation the female slaves submit."*
—LUCY STONE, ABOLITIONIST

*Margaret Garner, Maplewood
Farm, Richwood, Ky.*

Look at me and my swollen belly.
Look at my pale pale skin.
Look at this scar 'cross my face.

Don't call me Murderer.

My slave name is Next.
Look at my children.
You think they look like Massa Gaines too?

Step back from all this.
Stop eyeballing me and the sharp sharp blade.
Take a closer look   at the white men.

The older Gaines, who is also my daddy,
sold me to his brother, which means my uncle
has kept me barefoot and with child
since I was barely fifteen. I got three at my waist.
One on my hip. And one more in my belly
right now.

But don't count the children.
Look at the scars on my face.
These ain't from my husband's hand.

I spared my baby girl not from *this* life
but from *my* life.
You saw how much she look like me.

Half the lawyers think
this whole trial be not about murder
but if we be a people or property.

But it take another woman like Miss Lucy
to understand that it really be
about something else,
something much worser than taking a life,
or 'knowledging one,
about making a woman's body your smokehouse
and root cellar,
about believing her sore sore plum
is your fresh fruit.

That's all I gots to say.

AFTER MY DECEASE, A LAST WILL AND TESTAMENT

I give and bequeath all my silver ware and plate
of every description, also all my beds, bedsteads,
bed clothes, and the remaining household and kitchen furniture
to be split equally
amongst my daughter and 3 sons.

I give and bequeath to my daughter Nancy
my fortepiano
and also my negro woman Grace
and her youngest daughter Harriet.

I give to my son John
all my pictures
and also my negro boy Alfred,
son of the above mentioned Grace.

I give to my son James
my negro girl Sally
daughter of the above mentioned Grace.

And to Charles, I give my negro boy Wesley.

Should the said Grace or any of her increase
or any of the 48 slaves of mine
which shall become the property
of any of my children
prove troublesome and unmanageable

then it is my wish that such slave or slaves
so offending shall be sold
and the proceeds of such sale or sales
be appropriated to the purchase
of other servant or servants
to supply the place or places of those sold.

In witness where of I have hereunto set my hand
and affixed my seal this seventh day of December
in the year of our Lord 1857.
Signed, sealed and acknowledged

—MATILDA BURKS

MOTHER TO MOTHER

I believes you believes
this ink and paper testament
show off your love for your children
and how generous you can be.
And that may be so.

But it easy to be generous
when you gone.

What use a dead body got
with silver and slaves?

While I thank you
for the giving over a my Harriet
with me, I feel no such kindness for
the plowing up of the rest a my children.

And the added threat a being sold away
for daring to say anything
but yes ma'am and yassa boss
have me dreaming a swinging
the back a my hand
and fixing my own seal.

You can bind all my increase,
you can sell South my ungrateful tongue,
but you can't never give away my dreams.

A PINCH OF SEASONING

There was something about the way
Eliza's neck moved when she heard music
playing, especially a banjo,
and the inability to not move her feet
or dance in her seat.

When she turned her head a certain way
and grinned, especially when the sun
had kissed her face or other Fancy Girls
were standing nearby, there was something

on but off   like white pepper in your grits,
paprika in a stew. You couldn't really see it,
but once you tasted it   you knew   it was
definitely   there.

TEAMSTER

Six months after so-called emancipation,
the Union ordered the *impressment,*
the hired labor
of 6,000 male negroes
between sixteen and forty-five
in Central Kentucky.

Who else gonna build the roads?
Who else gonna dig the trenches?
Who else gonna raise the forts?
Who else gonna shoe and groom the horses?
Who gonna carry the heavy equipment,

wash, cook, and nurse for thousands of men?
Who else gonna drag an' burn the dead mules?
Who else gonna collect they fallen?

They didn't want us to shoot they guns,
but didn't mind if we carried the bullets.

SILENT PARTNER

I learn today that mama,
being property,
was massa's investment.

That taken all together,
the only thing more valuable
than us was the land.

That like the land, I, too, was property
and also my mama's interest
—same as her increase.

I was the bonus massa got
for investing in my mama.

He like investing so much
his wife say my green eyes
be *interesting,* by which I think
she mean—familiar.

I guess they had to sell mama
to profit, to save face,
to compound his interests,
but to multiply my loss.

BECAUSE I AM A MAN

Lewis Hayden

Bondage taught me that our dead son's cold grave
would always yield more peace than the horror
forced upon us by the ghost of the son sold away, forever.

Because I am a man with conviction, when we escaped
Lexington through stations in Ohio and on to Canada,
it only seemed right to settle in Boston, to commit
to providing shelter and protection for others,
and to aid as many travelers as possible.

Because I am a man with no son I can ever touch again,
our Boston boardinghouse was more than a way station.
It was a chance to spoon bowls of freedom soup,
to fluff pillows for the heads of every refugee child,
as if still tucking in my own, then standing watch
over their first peaceful night's sleep.

Because I am a man shredded by sorrow and unafraid
of death, I keep a keg of dynamite tied to a long fuse
in my basement.

Freedom, yours and mine, is a right I would gladly pay for
with my life, because I am   a man.

GRAPEVINE

Elijah P. Marrs

I brer rabbit into Simpsonville
so I can be the turtle coming back.
The horses know they way home,
so I use the extra time
to open Massa's newspapers
and read every word I can.

I unfold it with the tips of my fingers
and run my eyes 'cross
all the loud words first.
Like book faces and good preachers,
the big words tell you up front
what the story fixing to say.

Just 'cause folks in bondage don't get the paper
don't mean we don't want the news.

I practice my telling with a bit more spice
than when reading quietly to myself.
I promise to bring the stories,
but they expect me to bring the pictures too.

White folks think we don't know
what Lincoln say and do,

that the war being fought most everywhere else
'bout to find its way here too.

Just cause colored folk don't get the paper
don't mean they won't get the news.

TELEGRAM TO RECRUITS FROM THE PRESIDENT, AUGUST 1864

I told General Grant you must be his
canine teeth. You must bite like your
very freedom depends on it. I must
preserve the Union. I cannot win this war
without colored soldiers. I hope to have God
on my side, but I must have   Kentucky.

TELEGRAM TO LINCOLN FROM KENTUCKY USCT, AUGUST 1864

Thanks for finally taking
slave owners off the teat.

.

WHY I DON'T STAND

Oh, the sun shines bright
On my old Kentucky home,
  $1200 to $1250 DOLLARS! FOR NEGROES!!
'Tis summer, the darkies are gay.
  The undersigned wishes to purchase
  A large lot of Negroes
Well, corn top's ripe
  For the New Orleans market
And the meadow's in the bloom
  I will pay $1200 to $1250 for No. 1 young men
  and $850 to $1000 for No. 1 young women.
While the birds make music all the day.
  In fact, I will pay more for likely NEGROES
Weep no more, my lady
Oh, weep no more, today
  Than any other trader in Kentucky.
We sing one song
  My office is adjoining the Broadway Hotel
For my old Kentucky home
  On Broadway, Lexington, KY
For my old Kentucky home far away.
  Where I or my Agent can always be found.

FREDERICK DOUGLASS RECRUITS

Are Freemen less brave than slaves?
Colored men, enter the army, now!
Defend this country and her honor.
Enlist and take up arms against our
former masters. Fight for your families!
Generations of us have suffered under the
horrors of slavery. If we wish to be free
we must join in fighting the battles
of Liberty. Know that it is now or never!
Let us die as Freemen—not live as slaves.
Men of color, brothers and fathers, let
nothing deter you from joining this cause.
Our enemies have made this country believe
people of color are cowards. Quit feeding
those falsehoods. Rise up! Strike now
and enlist for three years of service. If we
march under the banner of the United States,
victory will be won. Come, let us prove
we are worthy, exceptional, and yearning
to fight zealously for our Freedom.

MOTHER MAY I?

Randall X Edelen, Company G,
125ᵗʰ U.S. Colored Infantry

Took almost four years
and a whole lot a dead, white bodies
to figure out they needed Kentucky
to win the war.

In March of '65 the gov'ment
said joining the Union Army
guaranteed freedom for each new soldier
and our families too.

Come April, I found my way to Lebanon
an signed my mark in ink for my Mary
and our John, Susan, William, Sallie,
Daniel, Scott, and Silas.

I'm sure Miss Jane felt like
she been robbed
losing nine slaves all at once
with the power of my *X*.

I know she had some unkind words
for good ol' Lincoln and the Gov'nor
who only offered her $300

for what them called compensated
'mancipation.

Knew she'd be fit to be tied so,
I didn't ask.
I enlisted   without consent.

BLUE SUMMER

Pvt. Henry Clay Walker,
12th U.S. Colored Heavy Artillery

If every single blade a grass in a field
stood in line and put on a new cap and boots
it might come close to helping you picture
how many of us showed up that summer.

I didn't care if I had to stand behind
all the bluegrass in the state,
by the time we all put on blue wool jackets
you could no longer see the weeds.

MEN OF COLOR

To Arms! To Arms!

NOW OR NEVER

This is our golden moment! The Government of the United States calls for every Able-bodied Colored Man to enter the Army for the

THREE YEARS' SERVICE!

AND JOIN IN FIGHTING THE

BATTLES OF LIBERTY AND THE UNION

A new era is open to us. For generations we have suffered under the horrors of slavery, outrage and wrong; our manhood has been denied, our citizenship blotted out, our souls seared and burned, our spirits cowed and crushed, and the hopes of the future of our race involved in doubt and darkness. But now our relations to the white race are changed. Now, therefore, is our most precious moment. Let us rush to arms!

FAIL NOW, & OUR RACE IS DOOMED

On this soil of our birth. We must now awake, arise, or be forever fallen. If we value liberty, if we wish to be free in this land, if we love our country, if we love our families, our children, our home, we must strike now while the country calls; we must rise up in the dignity of our manhood, and show by our own right arms that we are worthy to be freemen. Our enemies have made the country believe that we are craven cowards, without soul, without manhood, without the spirit of soldiers. Shall we die with this stigma resting upon our graves? Shall we leave this inheritance of shame to our children? No! a thousand times No! We WILL Rise! The alternative is open to us. Let us rather die freemen than live to be slaves. What is life without liberty? We say that we have manhood; now is the time to prove it. A nation or a people that cannot fight may be pitied, but cannot be respected. If we would be regarded men, if we would forever

SILENCE THE TONGUE OF CALUMNY

Of Prejudice and Hate, let us Rise Now and Fly to Arms! We have seen what

VALOR AND HEROISM

OUR BROTHERS DISPLAYED AT

PORT HUDSON AND MILLIKEN'S BEND,

Though they are just from the galling, poisoning grasp of slavery, they have startled the World by the most exalted heroism. If they have proved themselves heroes, cannot WE PROVE OURSELVES MEN?

ARE FREEMEN LESS BRAVE THAN SLAVES

More than a Million White Men have left Comfortable Homes and joined the Armies of the Union to save their Country. Cannot we leave ours, and swell the Hosts of the Union, to save our liberties, vindicate our manhood, and deserve well of our Country. MEN OF COLOR! the English, the Irish, the French, the German, the American, have been called to assert their claim to freedom and a manly character, by an appeal to the sword. The day that has seen an enslaved race in arms has, in all history, seen their last trial. We now see that

OUR LAST OPPORTUNITY HAS COME

If we are not lower in the scale of humanity than Englishmen, Irishmen, White Americans, and other Races, we can show it now.

MEN OF COLOR, BROTHERS AND FATHERS!

WE APPEAL TO YOU!

By all your concern for yourselves and your liberties, by all your regard for God and humanity, by all your desire for Citizenship and Equality before the law, by all your love for the Country, to stop at no subterfuge, listen to nothing that shall deter you from rallying for the Army. Come Forward, and at once Enroll your Names for the Three Years' Service.

STRIKE NOW!

And you are henceforth and forever FREEMEN!

E. D. Bassett,	Rev. J. Underdue,	Frederick Douglass,	Rev. J. C. Gibbs,	Elijah J. Durh,	James Needham,	Daniel Colley,
Wm. Whipper,	John W. Price,	P. J. Armstrong,	Daniel George,	John P. Burr,	Rev. Elisha Weaver,	J. C. White, Jr,
D. D. Turner,	Augustus Dorsey,	J. W. Simpson,	Robert M. Adger,	Robert Jones,	Ebenezer Black,	Rev. J. P. Campbell,
Jos. McCrummell,	William D. Forten,	Rev. J. B. Trusty,	Henry M. Cropper,	O. V. Catto,	Rev. William T. Catto,	Rev. W. J. Alston,
A. S. Cassey,	Rev. Stephen Smith,	S. Morgan Smith,	Rev. J. B. Reeve,	Thos. J. Dorsey,	James B. Gordon,	J. P. Johnson,
A. M. Green,	N. W. Depee,	William E. Gipson,	Rev. J. A. Williams,	I. D. Cliff,	Samuel Stewart,	Franklin Turner,
J. W. Page,	Dr. J. H. Wilson,	Rev. J. Boulden,	Rev. A. L. Stanford,	Jacob C. White,	David B. Bowser,	Jesse E. Glasgow,
L. R. Seymour,	J. W. Cassey,	Rev. J. Asher,	Thomas J. Bowers,	Morris Hall,	Henry Minton,	

U. S. Steam-Power Book and Job Printing Establishment, Ledger Buildings, Third and Chestnut Streets, Philadelphia.

II

"Any negro taken in arms against the Confederacy
will immediately be returned to a state of slavery. Any
negro taken in Federal uniform will be summarily
put to death. Any white officer taken in command
of negro troops shall be deemed as inciting servile
insurrection and shall likewise be put to death."

—PROCLAMATION OF THE CONFEDERATE CONGRESS

PALISADE PICKET FENCE SPEAKS

You'd never believe these grounds,
perfectly seated to seize the Cumberland Gap,

invade Tennessee, and protect the only bridge
between here and the state capital,

would instead lay siege to onyx men being chattel,
become a bridge to their first real freedoms,

provide a new home for recruits and their families.
You don't know how wise a choice that was

until you gaze across at the cliffs from the south
side and up at my high rock head and shoulders.

It's like God started building the perfect refuge
then left it up to his children to make it so.

GROVE

This was the first time
we really look at each other
and not be able to tell
who master the cruelest
who sorrow the deepest
who ground been the hardest to hoe.

We was lined up like oaks in the yard
standing with our chins up,
proud chests out, shoulders back,
and already nervous stomachs in.

We was a grove wanting to be a forest,
ready to see what kind of wood we made from.

The only thing taller or straighter
than us be the boards
holding up the barracks at our backs,

though most our feets feel pigeon-toed
and powerful sore
from marching back and forth, every day,
for what seem like more miles
than we walked to get here.

It take more than pride to stand still
'neath these lil' hats not made for shade.

Soldiering ain't easy, but it sure beats
the bloody leaves off a bondage.

DAMNED NORTHERN AGGRESSORS

Warren Wiley, Woodford County

Yes, abolitionists play high and mighty,
but they money is in the bank.
Mine is in dese niggers.
They want to take coins right out of my pocket,
turn my wealth into ghosts,
leave my corn rottin' in the field,
expect me to slop my own hogs,
send me crawlin' to the po' house.

I have read
from the bible to all my property.
All I expect in return is an honest day's work,
and no sass.
I kick my dawg. I whip my mules.
Why wouldn't I beat a darkie caught idle
on the farm? It's hard work keeping this many
lazy niggers in line.
If I had the energy I had in my younger years
I'd beat 'em all twice a day.

When I catch my servant Patsey staring out
at the nigger soldiers that marched by,
I think of her sorry, no-count husband
who run off, enlisted, and got hisself kilt.
Our hard-earned money was just marching

down the road whistling John Brown.
I was so angry I had to strip her
and beat her good.

I swung the cowhide for every northern sumbitch
I ever met. I swung it again for every nigger soldier
that signed up to kill whites.

I was so angry I had to beat the black off her.
I beat that gal 'til I was too tired to raise my hands.
Then I felt a little better.

Nothing says obey or makes it clear, exactly
who is the boss, like a slap 'cross the face.

—If you don't believe me ask my wife.

THE FIRE LAST TIME

Patsey Leach, U.S. Colored Troops
widow, Camp Nelson, March 25, 1865

Don't think white men truly know God from
the devil, cause that not the first time massa Wiley serve

Revelations and my nakedness on the same plate.
Never knowed a bible thumper to curse and damn

his God a full sermon long and with so much pepper
'fore a biscuit, bowl or bible fly 'cross the room,

and have a unpleasant meeting with the wall
or a woman. Every time them beautiful rows of blue corn

danced by, turning marching directions and the sound
a that many boots into a choir, I found reasons to be

in the yard, or as close to a window as I dared light.
But ol' massa catch a storm in his body, and turn

redder than any fire I ever seen. He slammed the door
and took a ax to wood that don't need chopping,

stomped back inside and look for something heavier
to throw, before sending me to the cellar where there be

no rainbow signs, and to wait for what he plan be the end
a the world, but feet answer prayers too.

UNSALTED

Mount six hundred men and horses.
Lead them over a hundred miles.
Steal their mounts,
knock off their hats,
pepper them with jeers all the way.
Give them Enfield rifles,
not Spencer repeating carbines.
Point them at the enemy
who have the higher ground.
Marvel at how valiantly untrained men die.

Hastily retreat.
Leave the wounded in the mud.
Express disdain to learn
that the Confederates murder
all the abandoned negroes they find.

Enlist those that survive.
Name them
the 5th United States Colored Cavalry,
the thrice shat upon, the fightin' fifth,
men you will be honored to lead.

HARRIET

Call her Moses, Conductor,
already Legend.

Call her Nurse attending to open wounds.
Call her Thief, Grand Larcener, absconding with
over 700 pieces of property
in the Combahee Ferry Raid.

Call her Union Scout, Spy, Ear Hustler,
Invisible Thorn to white male arrogance
refusing to see her or the threat.

Call her Map Maker. Call her Compass.
Call her North Star. Call her the Secret Way Home.

Call her the Hammer and the Finger on the gun.
The Powder. The Bullet between freedom and death.
Nickname her Minty, the Original Emancipator.
Call her by her one true name, Freedom Now   or Else.

FIGHTIN' WORDS

Northern counties broke off
from their southern sisters
and became West Virginia.

East Tennessee's left arm
split from its right after it seceded.

Our southernmost belles held hands,
left the Commonwealth
and became the thirteenth state
in the Confederacy.

Whoever said Kentucky didn't take sides
never looked in the mirror and hated
what they saw,
didn't know what it meant
to wage war against yourself.

The bluegrass was never neutral.
It wanted slaves
or all the money they were worth.

Some wanted negroes unshackled,
but only if their masters
were in rebellion.

Others wanted Black soldiers to fight,
but not to earn white pay.

If the war between the states
wasn't over slavery,
it was about whether
we should work   for free.

CATCH ME IF YOU CAN

Pvt. Jesse Hopson, Company F,
108th U.S. Colored Infantry

They say that's me, standing at attention in the picture,
imitating a sycamore, feet booted, rooted to the ground.
Look like my hat and uniform, my same fingernails and hands.

They say the face look like me, but I can't be sure.
I was never so lucky as to own a mirror.
This the first and onliest picture of me I ever seen.

My feet are not moving, so you can't tell how fast I really am.
I coulda been a racehorse. Our whole company is a thundering herd.
Massa Hopson chased me through the swamps for a week.

Owned a whole county in west Kentucky tucked 'tween two rivers,
but he couldn't catch me, not even with hounds.
Water ain't nothing but a muddy track to a born runner.

The voice behind the box said, stand there and hold still.
So, I let the pop and flash of the camera try to catch me.
But he couldn't know how hard that was for a man like me

to stand there, like a log, as if ol' massa looking my way,
looking for something in the woods outta place, something
moving, something he think he own, but it's just the sound of hooves.

MUTINY

Cornelius Taylor, Company M,
12th U.S. Colored Heavy Artillery

is just a fancy word white officers
use when they bark
roll over, nigger! or *sit up and beg, boy!*
—and we don't.

They been the master them whole lives
and believe *Obey!* come natural
to colored men.

But some of us was already free.
Some of us could already write
our own name.
And some of us just have a hard time
being talked down at   like dirt
under somebody's polished boot.

Most colored men done mutinied
in our minds and in our hearts
so many times since we joined
this great unshackling
it's a wonder our dress blues ain't dark gray.

We sleep with death every night
knowing Johnny Reb gone kill us

if they catch us in these colors
whether we lay down our arms or not.

Rolling our eyes, sucking our teeth,
and not biting our tongues
is just fleas on a rabid dog,
not the giant head foaming at the mouth
and certainly not   the fangs.

HOW SALT WORKS

when we retreated   we was following orders
                        leavin' them
ashamed and beaten   on that cold hard ground
so many miles away   in such cruel weather
                    meant abandonment
we were full of loss   leavin' them 'cross the lines
turning our backs on our own   with nothing to cover their bodies
it would be hard to survive   we remounted our horses
knowing they would die   we rode back without them
                    at Camp Nelson
                    we shed some tears
                then offered them a monument
we etched their names in stone   but left them no protection
had we been this cruel before   it felt like déjà vu

at the salt works   it felt like   we just threw them away.

BIRD WATCHING

Sgt. Maj. Charles Singer,
107th U.S. Colored Infantry

I was an educated businessman
from Covington, Kentucky
before I was mustered into the infantry.
Many of my fellow soldiers spent time
around the fire or on guard duty
debating the intricacies of our uniforms,
especially the itch of wool, the pinch of new shoes,
and the parade of wings.

I have eloquently defended the majesty
and the fierceness of the beautiful bald eagle,
especially the large one we wear
across our shoulder strap. To many an old soldier,
fresh out of bondage, the proud bird looking
backwards harkens to the Sankofa,
a important reminder to learn from our mistakes.

But the younger more skeptical brethren,
who question and challenge everything,
said they only loved one bird, the chicken—roasted,
and refuse to shine anything.
They believe when bullets start looking for a home,
it's just a big target in the center of our chest.

Later, in the dark, I consider our heated debate,
rub my thumb across the emblem on my
breastplate and wonder which one of us is wrong.

COST OF EQUALITY

Pvt. Allen W. King, Company B,
122nd U.S. Colored Troops

Decidin' anotha man can serve as you
is not the same as thinkin' he is your equal.

Of course, being anotha man's servant
is not the same as servin' for that man.

By the same, I don't means rich and white, I means
when docta John Clemens decided not to honor the draft

rather than sendin' a white man off to die
he purchased me to provide that service in his place.

It's one thing to wear another man's tight boots 'n hat
but it's something different to try on his fate.

OF COURSE

Margaret Garner

I'm not surprised so many of our men
enlisted, give over they lives
to see they mothers and families free.

No matter who they daddies be
they come here through Black mamas.
We made 'em all, mule mean and molasses.

That kinda love and pluck and sacrifice
could only come from us.
Same for that kinda strength.

We only have a few seasons to pour
so much iron and oak into them
no slaver could ever beat it out.

But they shoulda mustered me too.
It take gumption to give over your life.
It take even more to take one.

LOAD IN NINE TIMES

John Burnside, Company K,
124th Regiment, U.S. Colored Troops

Load!   I wonder
    Sit butt of musket on the ground.
Handle cartridge!   if I look down
    Pull paper cartridge from box.
Tear cartridge!   the business end
    Use teeth to rip top off.
Charge cartridge!   of my musket
    Put gunpowder in its mouth,
        add round.
Ram cartridge!   and see ol' Massa
    Pull metal rod from gun.
    Push it down the throat of musket.
Return rammer!   standing there
    Return metal rod.
Prime!   if I will hesitate
    Cock gun and seat cap.
Shoulder arms!   or remember
    Wait for orders.
Ready!   how many times
    Squeeze the trigger.
  Aim!   he beat my wife
    Fire!

WE WILL PROVE OURSELVES MEN

Sewn on the regimental flag of
the 127ᵗʰ U.S. Colored Troops

I don't look to the stars and stripes
nor the eagle for mustard

like the white officers
and some of my free brothers do.

I think on the slender fingers
that stitched our proud colors

snapping in the wind,
the same steady hands

that last held me close,
and pray they hold me again.

That's why I'm willing
to trade bullets in a cloud.

Some confuse our bravery and courage
with our love for our women,

but many of us just eyeing that flag
and trying our best to get back home.

GOLDEN SHOVEL FOR MATILDA DUNBAR

Paul Laurence Dunbar

I wish, but I can't say there was ever such a thing as a *we*.
I know papa wore his eagle buttons longer than he would wear
the mantle of husband or father. Who could know which of the
demons, enslavement or war, would break him, make him mask
himself, refuse the generosity and love you had to offer, that
you poured so generously onto me? A childhood filled with grins
is what I remember most, though marked with his absence and
his unkindness towards you. He left me with only the half-lies
about his exploits during battle. When he recalled and told it
he tried to disguise all the sorrow songs and grieving that hides
beneath even the most musical of tongues, deep up under our
laughter. You always wanted to see joy in my eyes and cheeks
or a book in my hand. You smiled at my fatherless dreams and
reminded me to listen to how the music in his story shades,
protects, and warms the belly of its listener, always making our
sad father, our *gallant colored soldier*, more heroic in my eyes.

MALE CALL

"Let it hasten to those who wait for tidings."

*Pvt. Edward Francis, Company
B, 114th U.S. Colored Infantry*

I was a fool to believe the money
in the letter I sent back home to my wife
wouldn't up an' run off or get lost.

I always pray the words straight
after the white lady scribble across
the page in my voice then sign *E. Francis.*

If I close my eyes, when my mail
return an' is read out loud for me
I can almost see and hear her

lining her words up like she herself
sitting there, warming me like this fire.
I imagine the dancing tongue of the flames

is her voice an' the sparks that shoot up
is her little laugh. Then I open my eyes
and stare at a blazing hot ember

and pretend she givin' me *that* look
'til the glow softens an' burns out.
It's them moments more than anything

that make me want to learn to scribble.
That an' not trusting these Christian
letter writers with the words every man

want to whisper to his wife
when he miss her this much.

COLOR BEARER

Easy to explain why the man carrying colors
is always short and hard like me
and the line for the honor even shorter.

A colored man needs a damn good reason to walk
into battle carrying a flag instead of a musket or pistol.

He can't cut and run when his brothers don't
hear the bugle call. They look to him to show the way.

To move forward, straight and true, while bullets
and cannon smoke fill the air all around you
takes something special.

Some believe it's heart. Some call it iron stomach,
and a strong belief that God will be our shield.

Others think a willingness to be the bearer means
a man be part crazy, up to his ears in don't-give-a-damn,
or got nobody waiting for him at home, but
only fools signed up expecting to get back there.

We are surrounded by death on every side. We just have
to choose which way we gone turn an' greet him.

TWO SOLDIERS WHO CAN'T SLEEP TELL JOKES

White Captain say to a colored recruit,
"Tell me a joke, boy."
The recruit say, "What's a joke, Sir?"
Cap'n say, "You know, a little story
'bout life that make somebody laugh."
The recruit say, "I been a slave all my life.
I ain't had nothing to laugh about."
Cap'n get mad an' say, "That can't be true.
I hear you niggers singing and laughing
all night long in the barracks. What's
so damn funny out there?" The recruit scratch
his head and think for a minute and finally
say, "Well sir, it probably sound like laughing
to you, but we is mostly just crying."
Cap'n say, "Crying? What the hell y'all got
to cry about today? Yesterday y'all was all slaves."
The recruit say, "Oh, we ain't forgot about
yesterday, Sir, and we ain't too tore up about today,
but we fulla tears about tomorrow."
Cap'n say, "What the hell's happening tomorrow?"
Recruit say, "That's just it Sir. We don't know
neither."   And after a while they both laugh,
a little.

BOOGEYMAN

I don't believe in ghosts or haints or boo hags,
but I know there be real monsters that walk
among us.

We seen our brothers
catch a face full a musket fire, get run clean
through with bayonets, and cut in half
with cannonballs and not flinch.

But whisper Massacre at Saltville or the ugliness
at Poison Springs or Fort Pillow
to any colored soldier and he will shiver
and throw salt over his shoulder right there.

At Tennessee and Kansas they gave no quarter.
At the salt works in Virginy they killed unarmed
captured and wounded soldiers,
some still laying in hospitals beds.

It one thing to go to battle against another man.
It another to be hunted, to be treated
like wild game, to not be killed in self-defense
but purely for sport, just to please the devil.

SIMPSONVILLE

Pvt. Samuel Trueheart, Company E,
5th U.S. Colored Cavalry

It was cold, snowy, bitter weather like
the heart of winter in Kentucky can be.

When the guerillas attacked that morning
the lone white officer was in town,
conveniently replacing the boots
he had been tricked out of the night before.

We had a fat herd of cattle between us
on the trail to Louisville moving towards
what was supposed to be their slaughter,
not ours, when the darkness at Saltville
returned like a ghost.

Nine hundred head of cattle don't know
how to sneak down a country road.
Eighty ex-slaves didn't either.

TWO SOLDIERS WHO CAN'T SLEEP COMPARE SCARS

My massa was so cruel
he stumble out to the cabins
and make the husbands
sit on the porch and listen
while he ride our wives.

My massa was so cruel
when my little yella girl skip over
and ask, "will you be my daddy?"
he turn her over and whisper,
"I already am."

EVERY PAGE A MILE

*E. Belle Mitchell, Camp
Nelson Refugee School*

I was born free. What I learned in books
helped me remain so, taught me to insist
that others cross the River Jordan too.

Thanks to the Bible, many of my people
tied literacy to their salvation.
Their real freedom was waiting for them
in a heaven filled with bookshelves.

It was my honor to teach the families
of brave colored soldiers at the refugee school.
To witness them on their journey to learn.
To be reminded of how reading and discussing
books was like a new pair of traveling shoes.

CHILDREN'S SONG

E. Belle Mitchell, Camp
Nelson Refugee School

What a joy it was to unshackle
their imaginations, to see something
different start to glow in their eyes.

Miss Mitchell, Miss Mitchell,
why it called hiss
story if it about us too?

Miss Mitchell, we hear the white teachers
won't eat with you. Is it because you Black
or cause you was already free?

Miss Mitchell, I been up all
night countin' all the new places
and things you put in my head.

Miss Mitchell, listen to me cast a spell;
M-Eye-Crooked letter-Crooked letter-
Eye-Crooked letter-Crooked letter-Eye-
Humpback-Humpback-Eye.

Their song is a church bell ringing.

TWO SOLDIERS WHO CAN'T SLEEP MAKE PLANS

After the war is over
if you could have tea
with Abe Lincoln's wife
in that white house,

some peach brandy
served by your old massa's
missus in they parlor,

or a drank a whiskey
with Harriet Tubman,
floating up the Ohio
on a steamboat,
which would you choose?

I'd trade everything for one sip a water
with my sista, who was sold
down river when I was just a pup.

LET MY PEOPLE GO

Minister Gabriel Burdett,
Company I, U.S. Colored Troops

As a man of Faith, I must share this truth:
The prayers and the God our captors offered,
in our state, seemed short on love and mercy.
We watched like sheep from Fork's Church gallery,
sang their pious hymns, then gathered again
in our own temple, veiled from prying eyes
and ears. Their thin cold songs were our first clue.
We wandered the wilderness long enough
to recognize His absence and His scorn.
Children of God do not need a Jordan.
We transformed the gospel into rivers,
swam all the way to heaven in our praise,
Where God is the lone master in His house.
Enslavement was not love. It was a sin.

But slavery was not sin in our state.
The Emancipation Proclamation
did not free a soul, let alone right wrong.
Lincoln wanted Kentucky's prayers or
at least no invocations with the South.
So it talked out of both sides of its mouth.
They needed six thousand men to work so,
our new master became the Union flag.
The government paid our owner's silver,
thirty pieces each to rent us like tools,
and called the new arrangement impressment.
When the federal wagon left the farm
I was torn from my family and church,
now part of the union, but still enslaved.

The enslaved parted ways with Ol' Pharaoh
when he commanded we be kept from books.
But he still wanted us to memorize
his Psalms. Singing required much attention
to words. Attention to words was a breath
from spelling and half the way to reading.
A captive who runs away and can't read
a signpost or a map is soon reclaimed.
He might run for days and not leave the page.
When they cite Exodus 5:1 to us,
they pretend it says that they are saviors,
and call all abolitionists Pharaoh.
They twist "that they may serve me" until it
is God commanding us to stay enslaved.

Owners believe God commands slaves to stay.
They will twist the scripture again until
the plagues on Egypt are not frogs or flies
but Union soldiers marching through the land
like locust. They had already proven
to those in bondage that their one true blight
had always been their religious excuse
for slavery. Our long days of darkness,
the auctioning off of our first-born sons,
and much worse, had already come to pass.
They are cutting off the ears of Black men,
tying them to trees, flaying them alive
for wanting to enlist, wanting freedom.
If we are indeed cursed, our plague is white.

The white man's new plague was re-enslavement
after the impressment plan was revoked.
But when victory needed more soldiers,
hesitant owners asked for the promise
of no sightings of uniformed ex-slaves.
Many resisted, showed their true morals
and nature, doubling down on savagery
that was now criminal by laws of war.
Once fugitive slave codes were stricken, we
were more than ready and willing to fight.
Our enlistment came with freedom papers,
a timely blessing, an answered prayer.
The church door to legal manumission
opened and we walked through by the thousands.

Thousands walked singing into camp that June
like the Israelites leaving Egypt,
no longer under the lash of cruel men.
The restrained praising done in seclusion
in the thick woods back in Garrard County
became a loud new church in the open.
Abolitionists and missionaries
showed us a different kind of white folk.
Though suspicious of Christianity,
freedmen joined in song almost every night.
Surrounded by many non-believers,
I was allowed to preach the Word again.
Not the master's Word about submission,
but *tell ol' Pharaoh let my people go.*

I had prayed that he let my people go.
Then, I prayed that He let us join the fight.
The men I preached to at night, fingers itched
to prove Douglass right, on the battlefield.
Though they still heard whispers about Pillow,
they were not ready for Saltville's horror.
These colored troops had not been mustered in
when they were armed and ridden into hell.
Their forced retreat left wounded men behind.
Ten colored soldiers were killed in action.
The forty-six abandoned lay bleeding
until the rebels came for them at dawn.
It was hard to hear about how they died.
Now I pray for peace for their kith and kin.

It is not God who commands kith and kin
of the now enlisted men, out of camp
and into the cold winter wilderness
without coats, or shelter over their heads.
These soldiers will want to know where He was
when women and children were shivering,
when the frailest among them froze to death.
I could not convince them this was God's will,
that this was part of a Grand Plan for us.
But as the Darkness crawled among the men
with whom I both fasted and prayed, He moved
mountains. The families were let back in,
given warm blankets, hot food, and fresh bread,
finally treated fairly, with respect.

If a white man respects all my people
and is not the good Lord's shepherd, John Brown,
he could only be minister John Fee.
Most slave captors in Kentucky loathed him,
and with reason. But I dare you to show
me another devout servant willing
to ring the Freedom Bell with all his might,
to want us to have schools as well as churches,
to pray that those in bondage take up arms
against those who would deny liberty.
Who else would pray with us before we rode
off to battle? Pray for our safe passage?
Pray for God to be our shield? Pray we smite
slavery, dressed in Union uniforms?

The sight of ex-slaves, dressed in uniforms
piled into our first tents, hungry to learn,
with so much devotion, is heaven sent.
They recite the Lord's Prayer, together,
read verses aloud from the Old Testament,
study geography and arithmetic,
and are learning how to sew their own clothes.
I am grateful for the Lord's protection.
When I was first carried to Camp Nelson
I felt just like Daniel in the lion's den.
I fasted on vegetables and water,
and avoided the camp meat and strong drink.
I have prayed for His continued guidance.
I feel delivered when in uniform.

Deliverance dressed in blue uniforms
is a picture only God could have drawn.
It looks like we are marching on solid
ground, but we are planting our feet on Faith,
not in a country or a president,
but in the belief that what is waiting
for us on the other side of this war
or any test the Lord sees fit to give
is a chance to finally all be free.
We no longer run away to find it.
Our salvation is finally in reach.
We wake each day with minds set on just that.
And we march forward with Him on our side,
new words in our mouths, and guns in our hands.

Even with guns and victory in hand,
even with my wife and seeds at my side,
all my personal accolades were moot.
At war's end the Union proved more loyal
to those who fought hard to keep us enslaved,
sold our children, killed our brothers and sons,
than those who sacrificed their lives for her.
Our blessed refuge home, Camp Nelson,
the first truly free patch in Kentucky,
became an easy focus of hatred
after troops and protection were withdrawn.
Though heartbroken, most families chased out,
the whole camp taken apart board by board,
faithful, I remained, but no promised land.

Not reaching the promised land shook my faith.
I wish to have prayers of all of those
seeking victories we still hope to gain
in this present campaign that we are now
entering. And being entrusted with
this position as the elector for
Henry Clay's proud and boasted district,
once the very center of the slave trade,
clothed with all the rights of American
citizens and being placed here to stand
by the old flag and those who fought under it,
God being my helper, I pray for a new
battleground. I believe in the rule of law,
I tried politics, but the Lord knew best.

The good Lord knows, the only thing stronger
than our desire for freedom was white folk's
desire to deny it. The Methodists,
Congress, and Freedmen's Bureau tried but failed
to make real the freedoms we all fought for
in Kentucky, then they stole our children
with the Apprenticeship Act, ignored
the reign of terror waged by Ku Kluxers,
kept us landless, shackled to poverty,
forced us to bow and scrape, accept everything
white as right   or leave the state, so we did.
Folk found their way to ships and Liberia.
My family moved to Kansas. I gave
too much to meet my maker still oppressed.

As a man of Faith, I must share this truth.
Because slavery was not sin in our state
we found the need to escape from Pharaoh,
a false Moses who told us God said, Stay!
One of the white man's plagues was enslavement
and why thousands joined up at Camp Nelson.
I had prayed that he let my people go.
Is it not Him who commands faithfulness
and for white men to love and respect us?
I have witnessed ex-slaves, dressed in God's glow,
become our deliverers robed in blue.
Even with guns and victory in hand
not reaching the promised land shook my Faith.
But Lord knows, it also made me stronger.

WHAT ABOUT THE CHILDREN?

Camp Nelson group photo, 1864

Though I can't rightfully say
what a ref-u-gee is,
I reckon it's like dying
and going on to glory,
without all the dying parts.

Look at alla us chil'ren,
Newly alive, our grown-up life
interrupted, to go to school,
to pick the right letters,
not corn or hemp,
to finally learn
how to be real chil'ren.

Dressed up like lil' women and mens,
some a us lookin' like somebody granny,
we already bruised, sore-footed, and tired-eyed.

We even stand like old people,
tired, worn, an fulla sorrows,

spendin' us whole days
tryin' to squeeze a lil' light
into all our dark places.

TO BE TOOK

Camp Nelson group photo, 1864

Look again. Even the ghosts
of some of us
have gathered here
to be took by the camera

some ankles deep,
some hoverin' almost 'fraid
to touch the dirt
that still cradles our bodies
now all rags and worms

lingerin' down front, at the edge
of the pitcha,
crossin' ova from the otha side
stealin' a peek at a different life.

Guess ol' folks was right
when they'd scold us and say
"there'll be plenny time to play
—when you dead 'n gone."

CHECKOUT TIME

Randall X Edelen, Company G,
125th U.S. Colored Infantry

It was good money
if you lived to collect it.

I was luckier than most.
It took a strained back
to slow me down enough
to catch one a them fevers
that travel through camps
with bad water
and not enough clean places to shit.

More of us catched the runs
an died from disease
in hospital beds than from bullets.

When I had the cholera
they mark me present, but sick.

When I catched the bloody flux
they mark me present, but sick.

Somehow, I survived, though it costs
Me my livelihood.

It costs many more men their lives.
This is what them mean
when they say freedom ain't free.

HEIRLOOM SEEDS

We was the rich dark earth
plowed up with possibility,

'umble little kernels
that grew into tall stalks.

Oh, what a harvest
when our crop come in!

We fed our families first, ate our fill,
and saved bushels of seed corn,

knowing it would be up to us
to till the ground next season.

·

Information Wanted.

OF my daughter, Martha James. When last heard from was in Montgomery, Ala, but is supposed to have gone to Mobile. She formerly belonged to Dr. Barnett, Princeton, Ky., and was sold to Mr. John James, Nashville, Tenn., about nine years ago, since which time she has not been seen by me. Information of her will be thankfully received by her mother by addressing Colored Tennessean, Box 1150, Nashville, Tenn.

HANNAH BARNETT.

mar10-1m.

OF my son, Daniel, 15 or 16 years of age, who formerly belonged to Clinton Williams, Marshal county, Tenn., and subsequently to Harvey McRory. When last heard from was in Memphis, Tenn. I am at present living at Unionville, Bedford county, Tenn., where I can be addressed, or the desired information can be sent to the Colored Tennessean, Box 1150, Nashville, Tenn.

feb10-1m   ROBERT WILLIAMS.

OF our five children, whom we have not seen for four years. Their names are as follows, viz: Josephine, aged 20 years; Celia, aged 14 years; Caroline, aged 13 years; Ellen, aged 10 years, and Augusta, aged 8 years. They were in Charlotte, N. C., or at Rock Hill when we last heard from them.

Any information concerning these children will be thankfully received by their mother. Our address is, Augusta, Ga.

AUGUSTUS BRYANT,
LUTITIA BRYANT.

N. B.—These persons were formerly owned by John L. and Virginia Moon, ot Augusta, Ga.   nov4-3m

III

"The people of Texas are informed that, in accordance with a Proclamation from the Executive of the United States, all slaves are free."

— GENERAL ORDERS, NO. 3
DELIVERED ON JUNE 19, 1865 IN GALVESTON

THE BIG BREAKUP

We was more than a little salty to find out
we'd been emancipated mo' than two whole years,
that masta crawled home from the war and decided
to keep our freedom to himself.

I 'member the urge to just set down and do nothing
for a spell, just to see what it feel like.
Then they told us we can now get paid for our labor.

But when we find out how little money it was,
a handful of us decided what we wanted to do
with our freedom was go find our beloveds
that was sold off or had run away.

Most all of us had missing family we ain't seen
since who knows when and was willing to walk
to Kingdom Come and back just to hold them again.
Working for just enough to keep you alive or laboring
to put sore eyes on loved ones that made life
worth living was a easy choice.

What freedom come to mean was to finally own land,
to build our own schools and businesses,
to travel unrestricted, to simply enjoy the right to hold
the hands, wipe the eyes, and kiss the cheeks
of the people you loved most in this world.

To be able to close your eyes and rest while you pray
for the strength to make it through whatever God got next.

God bless every fallen soldier. So many fought
for our freedom. More than 23,000 Kentuckians.
This is our Jubilee. This is our Emancipation Day.
This be our glorious Juneteenth.

RECONSTRUCTION

While white folks fussed over
rebuilding a country
and they wealth,
we gathered our freed selves
into lil' groups and quilted something
out of the pieces they left of us.

How do you un-orphan a people?
How do you pick up
shattered black porcelain and make
a new set of dishes fit to eat off?

First thing we learn
is nobody's plates and cups
gonna match.
Second is   they don't have to.

Big mamas become our tables.
All the men and women we can touch
become chairs.

Family come to mean, everybody
under this roof is kin
who ever wake up here do they piece.

It didn't really matter who smoked
the meat, if we had it.

BIRTH OF A NOTION

Kilt snakes and stomped spiders
that I know didn't mean me no harm.
Been embarrassed that I was afraid,
and learnt to understand that my actions
come from a place where my worst
childhood fears and nightmares shacked up.

Seen all kinds of children, privileged and not,
lose something them value—a toy, a game, a dawg.
Turn beet red, fight off tears, have a anger well up
so powerful, it look like them just might bust.

Seen they grown selves lose something precious
and watch a uglier, even more bitter anger rise up,
multiplied, and them up and shoot the horse,
lash and beat the runaway—deny losing the war.

Seem to be a poison inside them, a darkness,
born into the world afraid of this little light a mine.

DON'T JUDGE ME

Hillary Johnson, Hodgenville,
Ky., October 21, 1865

I believe in law and order. I accepted
the congressional mandate that declared
I was no longer his master,
and his woman and children no longer
my property, but the law could not
deprive me of proprietorship
of the clothes on their backs.

When that nigger soldier carried them
past my fence line dressed in those shirts,
he willfully and without my permission
showed everyone what a low-down
thieving scoundrel he really was. Of course,
I had him arrested and jailed without bail.
He stole from me. He committed larceny.

He violated my rights as a property owner.
And I should know.   I'm the County Judge.

OUR GRIEVANCE

Colored Citizens of Frankfort,
Ky. Committee, April 11, 1871

Freedmen and women
of Frankfort write this appeal
to those in Congress

concerning soldiers
of the late rebel armies
who subvert the rights

guaranteed to us
by the great Constitution,
newly amended.

Night-riding white thugs
rob, whip, rape, burn out, and kill
whole Black families

while their protection
from violence and terror
is ignored, denied!

HENRY MARRS,
Teacher Colored School,
HENRY LYNN,
Livery Stable Keeper,

H. H. TRUMBO, *Grocer,*

SAMUEL DEMSEY,

B. SMITH,

B. J. CRAMPTON, *Barber,*

Committee.

1867-1868, DARK YEAR IN THE BLUEGRASS

A colored schoolhouse burned by incendiaries in Breckinridge.
Negro taken from jail in Frankfort and hung by a mob.

Negroes attacked, robbed, and driven from Summerville.
A Colored school exhibition at Midway attacked by a mob.

Negro shot at Morganfield. U.S. Marshal attacked, captured,
and threatened with death in Larue County by a mob.

Two negroes beaten by Ku-Klux in Anderson County.
House of Oliver Stone attacked by Mob in Fayette County.

A man hung by a mob near Coger's Landing in Jessamine.
George Rogers hung by a mob at Bradfordville.

Mary Smith Curtis, Margaret Mosby, and Silas Woodford beaten.
Cabe Fields, shot and killed by a mob of disguised men near Keene.

James Gaines, expelled from Anderson by Ku-Klux.
Noah Blankenship, whipped by a mob in Pulaski County.

Smith attacked and whipped by a mob in Nelson County.
William Pierce hung by a mob in Christian County.

William and John Gibson, hung by a mob in Washington County.
Sam Davis hung by a mob at Harrodsburg.

William Glasgow, killed by a mob in Warren County.
Jerry Laws and James Ryan hung by mob at Nicholasville.

Cummins, his daughter, and Adams killed by mob in Pulaski County.
House attacked by mob in Cornishville. Crasbaw killed.

BIRTH OF A NOTION, NO. 2

Lost sleep trying to understand fear
and hate wedded to violence.

Why it deemed acceptable
as retribution
for potential black defilement
of white women
or even the thought of such.

Yet, they stir up others with fears
a what them call "mongrels"
as if all these so-called half-breeds,
quadroons, and octoroons
up and made themselves.

Maybe there was something so sweet
in the mammy's milk they suckled,
they'd do anything to taste it again.

OATH KEEPER

"... solemnly swear or affirm that ... I will bear true faith,
and yield obedience to the Confederate States of America ..."
—CONFEDERATE ENLISTEE OATH

They call us night riders, desperadoes, and regulators,
but most of us is just soldiers, in disguise, still loyal.

What we do now is no less noble
than what we done during the fight we took to Yankees
at Perryville, Munfordville, or Paducah.

We ain't shooting *all* the colored, just the ones who still
got fight left after we try to teach 'em, they mouthy women,
and pickaninnies a lesson or two.

Nothing worse than proud darkies, thinking what happened
at Appomattox made them our equals, or that the end
a slavery meant the end of yes sir, yes ma'am, and no more fear.

Watching a colored farm or church or school in flames feels like
a battle won. And every time I see a uppity nigra strung up or
one shot down, it's our victory at Richmond all over again.

PROUD BOYS

How could we not be? We know the General
would be too. To see 200 strapping former Cavalry, still riding,

knowing how he dispensed justice at that beautiful Fort Pillow
where Tennessee peeks across the Mississippi into Arkansas.

We are committed to sending the same message. This land
is *our* land. We are armed and dangerous. We will put darkies

and all their sympathizers in their place. We still give no quarter.
They should be afraid. They should be very afraid.

EX-CONFEDERATE OFFICERS TOAST

I really miss the good old days.
I can't believe we are supposed to pay 'em to work.

I miss those days too. I offered a boy a dollar for a week's work,
and he refused. Said he was buying land with his bloody
soldier money and gonna work for hisself.

Well, I been thinking. If we can't chase 'em all off those farms,
what if we make it against the law for 'em to sell their crops
in the city. And to be unemployed?
We could call them vagrancy laws. Lock 'em up. Fine 'em.
And then hire 'em back from prison to do the same work.

You know my brother's the sheriff and my cousin runs the prison?

Damn, that's smart, but what if we declare 'em to be unfit,
take custody of their children and make 'em work for free
'til they turn twenty-one. We could call it an apprenticeship act
and say we're teaching 'em the art of farming and housekeeping.

You know my son is a lawyer and my uncle is the county judge?

Hell, that's even better, but don't the law say you have to teach
apprentices how to read and write?

Not if they're black.

Hell, I'm feeling better already, though the more I think on it,
we might have gone to war for nothing.
We could have just changed the laws.
Can we make it illegal to be free and not be white?

Hmm, let me ask my neighbor. You know he used to be Governor?

BIRTH OF A NOTION, NO. 3

"She lusted after their lovers . . ."
—EZEKIEL 23:20

Seen folks' faces flush red, a sweat come over them,
require a quick fan at the sight of a handsome bull
or stallion catching the scent of a broodmare in heat.

Seen big men hung from trees by little men more afraid
they was hung like beasts, pretending to protect
mothers and daughters with a noose or castration,

making bonfires out of the secret desires of their wives,
—devout sanctified Christians, very familiar with lust,
that claimed to have read and understood the Good Book.

Maybe they pored over Ezekiel, and it ignited some fears.
Maybe the violence and hatred against everything black
was just worry about truth or just wife control,

was just a twisted way of praying   and not talking
about their obsessions   with breeding.

AFFIDAVITS

Mary X Edelen, Civil War widow

Them make me scratch out a *X*
in ink   with two witnesses
on afta-Davids
to prove me and Randal was married.

I fetched afta-Davids
from every doctor still living
that examined
my husband's piles
and old man's bladder,
witnessed his pain,
and still doubted his suffering
while he rot from the inside.

Them even bade me make my mark
afta-David with more witnesses
to prove my Randal was dead and gone.

They made me *X* the page
with witnesses so many times
on so many pension papers
that though I can not read
or write a lick,
I come to recognize
my own name when I see it.

The fancy *M* on Mary come to look like
a woman keep changing her mind.
And the *E* them like to put on Edelen,
a tired old bitty in a bonnet
who done set herself down an quit.

I first think my mark look like
a tired ol' cross,
but after a while I come to see
a long sharp knife
like my Randal's old scabbard from de war.

BUFFALO SOLDIERS

John Wesley Burkes, Company B,
125th Regiment, U.S. Colored Infantry

This Kentucky boy
was on escort duty
in New Mexico
when Congress officially graced
Black troops
out west with the name.

But Black soldiers of the 9th Cavalry
and the 38th and 125th Infantries
had already earned it.

Some say it was simply our wooly hair
reminding Indians of their sacred beasts,
but them that know the truth
believe they saw something similar
in the spirit, character, nobility,
toughness, and power of both.

But maybe, they watched how the white world
looked at us and only saw our skins.

PENMANSHIP

Mary X Edelen, Civil War widow

i woulda knowed
who longhand was who
even if I didn't see 'em
scratch out they names
on the paper
to swear my *X* is mine.

my William be proud,
like his daddy
he address his letters as pretty
as he dress his self.
his ink ease off the quill
just as smooth

as words off his tongue,
but my Scott and his letters
seem to take the long way
'round, make big slow loops,
and care not if they spine
stand up straight or not.

my Will glides 'cross them lines
like they pretty hardwood floors
while my Scott,

more accustom to dirt,
seem half 'fraid to touch 'em.

BLACK LOVE DAY

We scraped together the fifty-cent fee,
then a bit more, for the certificate
and picked 'n carried over a lil' something
from our garden for the minister.

Now that we finally owned ourselves,
we put down the broom and jumped at the chance
to own our promises too.

We had practiced as much husbandry as owners
believed was profitable,

been forced to carry uninvited seed to fruition,
yet shared cabins or memories of a broom jumping
with somebody we choose on our own.

And no matter how long ago we figured out
how to have and to hold, to stand 'fore God
and say, I do, was mighty special.

A BLACK FATHER DREAMS A SON

Brig. Gen. Charles Young,
9th U.S. Cavalry Regiment

It was twelve miles to Maysville and the Ohio River and another
ten to Ripley. A runaway could escape from Mays Lick,
at night, head north, follow the smell of the river and make
the entire distance and crossing by sunrise. A determined one,
on horseback, like Gabriel Young, could make it in half the time.

Ignoring racism at West Point was easier knowing
my father survived slavery. He joined the 5th and risked his life
so our people would know freedom. I risk mine to protect it.

If his sacrifice and commitment freed my body, my mother's books
freed my mind. Her skirt was my first classroom.
Every big and small thing I've done began at their feet.

Though born into slavery in Kentucky, I learned to play piano
and violin, speak French and German, before becoming a teacher,
before graduating from West Point, before a career in the military,
and public service.

Growing up in Ripley showed me what this country could be.
What my parents instilled in me, and Wilberforce proved it.

I am America's promise, my mother's song,
and the reason my father had every right to dream.

TIMELINE

1833

The Kentucky legislature passes the NON-IMPORTATION ACT, which prohibits the importation of slaves into Kentucky by purchase.

September 18, 1850

Congress passes the FUGITIVE SLAVE ACT OF 1850, which provides for the seizure and return of runaway slaves, even if in a free state. The act also makes the federal government responsible for finding, returning, and trying escaped slaves. Fugitives can't testify on their own behalf, nor are they permitted a trial by jury.

October 17, 1859

Abolitionist John Brown leads a raid on the United States Arsenal at Harpers Ferry, as part of an effort to initiate a slave rebellion in the southern states.

1860

Maryland has 87,189 slaves, Missouri has 114,931, Kentucky has 225,483. Only Virginia and Georgia have more slaveholders than Kentucky.

April 1861

Confederates fire on Fort Sumter, South Carolina. Free African Americans in the North try to enlist in the Union Army but are turned away.

April 15, 1861

Lincoln declares an insurrection exists and calls for 75,000 troops. Virginia, Arkansas, North Carolina, and Tennessee secede.

May 1861

Governor Beriah Magoffin issues a FORMAL PROCLAMATION OF NEUTRALITY and advises Kentuckians to remain at home and away from the fight. He does not believe slavery is a "moral, social or political evil."

August 6, 1861

Congress passes and Lincoln signs the CONFISCATION ACT OF 1861, which permits the confiscation of property used to support the Confederacy, including enslaved people.

September 18, 1861

Neutrality ends. Kentucky enters the Civil War on the side of the Union.

November 18, 1861

Two hundred delegates of southern sympathizers pass an ORDI- NANCE OF SECESSION and establish Confederate Kentucky.

December 1861

CONFEDERATE KENTUCKY is admitted as the 13th state in the Confederate States of America. Bowling Green becomes the capi- tal. George W. Johnson is appointed governor. Governor Magoffin resigns and sides with the Confederacy. Over 25,000 Kentuckians join the Confederate Army.

July 1862

Congress passes the MILITIA ACT, which allows Black men to serve in U.S. armed forces as laborers.

July 17, 1862

Lincoln signs the 2nd CONFISCATION ACT, expanding previous terms allowing for broader seizure of Confederate property and the emancipation of enslaved people, and prohibiting the return of fugitive slaves. The act authorizes the president "to employ as many persons of African descent as he may deem necessary and proper for the suppression of the rebellion." On the same day, Congress passes the MILITIA ACT, which authorizes the president to employ Black soldiers and to emancipate their families.

September 22, 1862

Lincoln issues the PRELIMINARY Emancipation Proclamation.

October 29, 1862

African American soldiers skirmish with Confederates at Island Mound, Missouri.

January 1, 1863

The EMANCIPATION PROCLAMATION declares enslaved people in states in rebellion against the Union free, and authorizes the enlistment of Black troops.

May 1, 1863

The Congress of the Confederate States of America passes the RETALIATORY ACT, authorizing the execution of white officers of Black regiments and the execution or re-enslavement of Black soldiers.

May 22, 1863

The U.S. War Department issues GENERAL ORDER NO. 143 establishing the United States Colored Troops. 23,703 Kentucky African Americans respond to the call to arms.

May 21–July 9, 1863

Eight African American regiments take part in the Battle of Port Hudson, Louisiana, giving the Union complete control of the Mississippi River.

June 1863

The 4th U.S. Colored Field Artillery (Heavy), located in Columbus, Ohio, is the first to organize with African Americans from Tennessee and Kentucky.

June 20, 1863

Northwestern counties of Virginia break away from Virginia over the slavery issue and form WEST VIRGINIA, becoming the 35th state of the Union.

July 1, 1863

First Kansas Colored Volunteers fight in the Battle of Cabin Creek.

July 10–11, 1863

The 54TH MASSACHUSETTS VOLUNTEER INFANTRY becomes the first Black regiment to see combat when U.S. troops attack Confederates near Charleston, South Carolina.

July 30, 1863

Lincoln issues GENERAL ORDER 252 in response to Confederate mistreatment of Black soldiers, declaring, for any U.S. prisoner killed in violation of the laws of war, a Confederate prisoner will be killed in exchange.

November 19, 1863

The GETTYSBURG ADDRESS.

December 1863

Robert Smalls becomes the first and only African American to be commissioned captain in the U.S. Navy during the Civil War.

April 12, 1864

The Confederate cavalry under Nathan Bedford Forrest attacks and overwhelms the Federal Garrison at FORT PILLOW, Tennessee. Forrest's troops execute almost 300 mostly Black soldiers after they have surrendered.

April 17, 1864

General Grant forbids prisoner exchange talks to progress unless Confederate authorities agree to treat Black soldiers the same as white, and until Confederates release enough U.S. soldiers to make up for the large number of Confederates paroled at Vicksburg and Port Hudson.

June 13, 1864

SPECIAL ORDER NO. 20 allows enslaved persons to enlist into the U.S. Army without their owner's consent and be granted freedom, becoming the first path to legal emancipation in Kentucky. Over 14,000 men in the state enlist over the summer.

June 15, 1864

Congress passes a bill authorizing equal pay, equipment, arms, and healthcare for African American troops.

June 28, 1864

The FUGITIVE SLAVE ACTS are repealed.

July 6, 1864

GENERAL ORDERS, NO 24 orders all women, children, and elderly and infirm men removed from Camp Nelson, in Jessamine County, Kentucky, the largest training site for African American enlistees.

July 15, 1864

MINISTER GABRIEL BURDETT enlists for three years with Company I of the 114th USCT.

September 29, 1864

Battle of Chaffin's Farm, Virginia. Fourteen U.S.C.T. earn the Medal of Honor.

October 1864

Forty-six wounded African American soldiers from 5th and 6th U.S. Colored Cavalry are murdered in a post-battle massacre, some in their hospital beds, at SALTVILLE, VA.

November 22–24, 1864

Brig. Gen. S. S. Frye expels over 400 women and children from Camp Nelson and has their temporary shelters destroyed. Many freeze to death.

Dec 15, 1864

Adjutant General L. Thomas issues ORDERS NO. 29 requiring all camps enlisting Negroes to provide suitable housing and provisions for their families.

January 25, 1865

Dozens of 5th U.S. Colored Infantry stationed at Camp Nelson are killed in an ambush by Confederate guerillas in SIMPSONVILLE, Kentucky, while driving 900 head of cattle on the old Midland Trail (U.S. 60).

February 1, 1865

Abraham Lincoln signs the 13th Amendment, abolishing slavery throughout the United States.

February 12–June 2, 1865

125th U.S. Colored Infantry are the last African American troops to organize at Louisville.

February 24, 1865

The KENTUCKY GENERAL ASSEMBLY refuses to endorse the end of slavery and votes against ratification of the 13th Amendment, which abolished slavery except as punishment for crime.

March 13, 1865

The Confederacy's president Jefferson Davis signs a NEGRO SOLDIER LAW which authorizes the enlistment of enslaved men as soldiers.

April 9, 1865

Robert E. Lee surrenders to Ulysses S. Grant at Appomattox Courthouse, officially ending the Civil War.

April 14, 1865

President Lincoln is assassinated by actor John Wilkes Booth at Ford's Theater in Washington, D.C.

June 19, 1865

Enslaved African Americans in Texas are the last to learn of their emancipation. The day is celebrated thereafter as "Juneteenth."

August 1865

Members of the 12th USCHA are charged with MUTINY for protesting the treatment of one of their soldiers, Cornelius Taylor, at Fort Boyle, near Colesburg, Kentucky.

December 1865

Federal law forces Kentucky to emancipate enslaved people when the 13th AMENDMENT is approved by three-quarters of the states.

February 14, 1866

The General Assembly approves an act that legalizes the marriages of freedmen and authorizes Black ministers in good standing in recognized Negro churches to solemnize marriages.

February 16, 1866

The APPRENTICESHIP ACT binds formerly enslaved children to their former owners (boys until age 21 and girls until age 18) to be taught the art of housekeeping or farming. They each are to receive

50–100 dollars upon release, unless the child is taught to read and write.

December 20, 1867
The last United States Colored Troop unit is mustered out of the Army.

July 4, 1925
The first and only monument to some of Kentucky's African American Civil War soldiers is unveiled in Green Hill Cemetery, Frankfort.

March 18, 1976
Kentucky symbolically ratifies the 13th Amendment.

July 4, 1998
"The Spirit of Freedom," created by Louisville's Ed Hamilton, is unveiled on the mall in Washington, D.C. It includes 209,145 names of U.S. Colored Troops.

ACKNOWLEDGMENTS

Early versions of some of these poems appear on the website of Reckoning Inc. and in an exhibit at the Frazier History Museum alongside copies of the historical documents that inspired them. I am eternally grateful to George Wright and Amy Murrell Taylor, historians supreme who let me badger them with early drafts of these poems and shared their extensive knowledge so generously; Matthew Strandmark and Megan Mummey of the University of Kentucky Library Archives; Nana Lampton and the research team at Reckoning Inc., particularly Dan Gediman, Denyce Peyton, Abigail Posey, and Ron Coddington; Rachel Platt of the Frazier History Museum and her curatorial staff, Amanda Briede and Olivia Couch. I appreciate the assistance from Tim Talbott, Reinette Jones, and Kristine Yohe.

A special thanks to Marquette Milton, Historical Interpreter at the African American Civil War Museum. Thanks to Robert Bell, Scott Thompson, and Ed Hamilton for the inspirational eagle medallion. Thanks to Makalani Bandele, who served as wet nurse to my Heroic Crown. Thanks to Adrian Matejka, Carter G. Woodson Academy, and Gina Iaquinta for believing in these poems.

And my eternal gratitude to Shauna Melissa Morgan, who stole time from a very hectic schedule to provide a first edit and look these poems in the face.

NOTES

"Truth Be Told": The title comes from the opening line in Natasha Trethewey's title poem in *Native Guard*, Mariner Books, 2006.

"Accounting": The title comes from the 1850 U.S. Federal Census-Slave Schedules, District 1, Jefferson, Kentucky.

"After My Decease, a Last Will and Testament": This poem is inspired by the will of Matilda Burks. Kentucky Wills and Probate Records, 1774–1989.

"A Pinch of Seasoning": Eliza, who was said to be just 1/64 Black, was sold at Cheapside in Lexington to satisfy the debts of her deceased master and father. "Fancy Girls" refers to enslaved mulatto girls and women sold as concubines or prostitutes to wealthy patrons.

"Teamster": On July 1862, Congress passed the Militia Act, which allowed Black men to serve in the U.S. armed forces as laborers.

"Because I Am a Man": In 1863, Lewis Hayden, who escaped enslavement in Kentucky in 1844, persuaded his close friend, Massachusetts governor John Andrew, to push for and win the inclusion of Black men in the Union Army. Hayden subsequently was successful in helping set up the first Black regiment in the Massachusetts Union Army. In 1873, he became one of the first Black men elected to the Massachusetts legislature.

"Telegram to Recruits from the President, August 1864": The poem alludes to the quote "Hold on with a bulldog's grip" included in a decrypted telegram sent by President Lincoln to General Grant on August 17, 1864.

"Why I Don't Stand": The poem contains original lyrics from "My Old Kentucky Home, Good Night," published in 1853 by Stephen Foster, and text from a July 2, 1853 slave trade ad run by William F. Talbott.

"Frederick Douglass Recruits": Inspired by the 1863 printed broadsides recruiting men of color written by Frederick Douglass.

"Mother May I?" The closing line is taken from the comment written on the back of Edelen's April 12, 1865 Army Enlistment Card, "enlisted without consent."

"Blue Summer": 14,000 men enlisted over the summer of 1864.

"Grove": Based on a photo taken at Camp Nelson of troops standing at attention outside the Colored Soldiers Barracks.

"Damned Northern Aggressors": Inspired by an affidavit filed by Patsey Leach, a Kentucky soldier's widow, at Camp Nelson, March 25, 1865.

"The Fire Last Time": Alludes to James Baldwin's *The Fire Next Time*, which concludes with the line "God gave Noah the rainbow sign, / No more water, the fire next time!"

"Catch Me If You Can": Based on a photo of Pvt. Jesse Hopson, Company F, 108th U.S. Colored Infantry.

"Mutiny": Members of 12th USCHA were charged with mutiny for protesting the treatment of one of their fellow soldiers, Cornelius Taylor, in August 1865, at Fort Boyle, near Colesburg, Kentucky.

"How Salt Works": At Saltville, 46 U.S. Colored Cavalry, abandoned after a retreat, were massacred by Confederates, Oct 2–3, 1864. On Nov. 23, 1864, Brig. Gen. S. S. Fry gave orders for the expulsion of all Colored women and children from Camp Nelson. Many froze to death in the bitter cold weather. Affidavit of Joseph Miller, 26 Nov. 1864, filed with H-8 1865, Registered Letters Received, Series 3379, Tennessee Assistant Commissioner, Bureau of Refugees, Freedmen, & Abandoned Lands, Record Group 105, National Archives.

"Cost of Equality": Pvt. Allen W. King enlisted in Company B, 122nd U.S. Colored Infantry, Oct 1, 1864, as a surrogate for Mark Twain's cousin.

"Of Course": Margaret Garner was born a slave in Kentucky and escaped to freedom in Ohio. When recaptured, she killed her young daughter rather than see her returned to slavery.

"We Will Prove Ourselves Men": This title comes from the motto on the regimental flag of the 127th U.S. Colored Troops.

"Golden Shovel for Matilda Dunbar": Paul Laurence Dunbar's father, Joshua Dunbar, escaped slavery in Kentucky and served briefly in the 55th Massachusetts before enlisting in the 5th Massachusetts Colored Volunteer Cavalry, where he served until he was mustered out on October 31, 1865. The poetic form, the Golden Shovel, was created by Terrance Hayes.

"Male Call": The U.S. Christian Commission provided stationery and writing services for illiterate soldiers. The epigraph is from the letterhead of the stationery they used.

"Boogeyman": Champ Ferguson killed over 100 Union soldiers and was one of only two men found guilty of war crimes after the war, but not for Black soldiers he killed, only for a white one.

"Simpsonville": Twenty-two soldiers from Company E, 5th U.S. Colored Cavalry, were killed in an ambush by Confederate guerillas on January 25, 1865.

"Every Page a Mile": E. Belle Mitchell's parents were former slaves who bought their own freedom before her birth. She was educated at a private school in Danville, Kentucky, and in Xenia, Ohio. In fall 1865, John G. Fee, an AMA minister and abolitionist, hired Mitchell for her first teaching position as the first African American teacher at Camp Nelson's Refugee School.

"The Big Breakup": General Order No. 3, a proclamation freeing all slaves, was delivered on June 19, 1865, in Galveston, Texas, and celebrated since as Juneteenth or Jubilee Day.

"Our Grievance": The title comes from official grievances filed with Congress by organized Colored Citizens of Frankfort, Kentucky, on April 11, 1871.

"1867–1868, Dark Year in the Bluegrass": Based on an addendum filed with an official grievance that listed details of a multi-year campaign of domestic terrorism, mob violence, and lynchings in Kentucky.

"Proud Boys": Confederate general Nathan Bedford Forrest served as the first Grand Wizard of the Ku Klux Klan, 1867–69.

"A Black Father Dreams a Son": Charles Young, born in 1864 into slavery to Gabriel Young and Armenta Bruen in Mays Lick, Kentucky, was the first Black man to achieve the rank of colonel in the United States Army, and the highest ranking Black officer in the regular army until his death in 1922. In 2022, in recognition of his exemplary service and barriers he faced due to racism, he was posthumously promoted to brigadier general.

BIBLIOGRAPHY

Coddington, Ronald S. *African American Faces of the Civil War: An Album.* Johns Hopkins University Press, 2012.

Howard, Victor B. *Black Liberation in Kentucky: Emancipation and Freedom 1862–1884.* University Press of Kentucky, 2010.

Myers, Marshall, and Chris Propes. "'I Don't Fear Nothing in the Shape of Man': The Civil War and Texas Border Letters of Edward Francis, United States Colored Troops." *The Register—Kentucky Historical Society*, vol. 101, no. 4, 2003, pp. 457–78.

Roberts, Rita. *I Can't Wait to Call You My Wife: African American Letters of Love Marriage and Family in the Civil War Era.* Chronicle Books, 2022.

Sears, Richard D. *Camp Nelson Kentucky: A Civil War History.* University Press of Kentucky, 2002.

Smith, Gerald L., editor. *Slavery and Freedom in the Bluegrass State: Revisiting My Old Kentucky Home.* University Press of Kentucky, 2023.

Taylor, Amy Murrell. *Embattled Freedom: Journeys through the Civil War's Slave Refugee Camps.* University of North Carolina Press, 2018.

Thompson, Scott F., "'The Negro had been run over long enough by white men, and it was time they defend themselves': African-American Mutinies and the Long Emancipation, 1861–1974'" (2021). Graduate Theses, Dissertations, and Problem Reports. 8051. https://research repository.wvu.edu/etd/8051.

Trethewey, Natasha D. *Native Guard.* Houghton Mifflin, 2006.

Wright, George C. *Racial Violence in Kentucky 1865–1942: Lynchings Mob Rule and "Legal Lynchings."* Louisiana State University Press, 1996.

ILLUSTRATION CREDITS

PART 1

Page xiv

NC Runaway Slave Notices Project (uncg.edu)

NC Runaway Slave Notices Project (uncg.edu)

NC Runaway Slave Notices Project (uncg.edu)

PART 2

Page 26

Collection of the Smithsonian National Museum
of American History and Culture

PART 3

Page 82

Library of Congress, Chronicling Amer-
ica: Historic American Newspapers